Sepher Yezirah, A Book on Creation

Or, Jewish Metaphysics of Remote Antiquity

Translated by

Isidor Kalisch

First published in 1877

Published by Left of Brain Books

Copyright © 2023 Left of Brain Books

ISBN 978-1-396-32656-1

First Edition

All rights reserved. No part of this publication may be reproduced, distributed, or transmitted in any form or by any means, including photocopying, recording, or other electronic or mechanical methods, without the prior written permission of the publisher, except in the case of brief quotations permitted by copyright law. Left of Brain Books is a division of Left Of Brain Onboarding Pty Ltd.

PUBLISHER'S PREFACE

About the Book

"The Sepher Yezirah is the central text of the Kabbalah, in which the doctrine of the 'mother letters' is expounded, and the associations between the other letters and the 'tree of life' are exposited."

(Quote from sacred-texts.com)

CONTENTS

PUBLISHER'S PREFACE
PREFACE 1
   CHAPTER I. 7
   CHAPTER II. 18
   CHAPTER III. 24
   CHAPTER IV. 29
   CHAPTER V. 38
   CHAPTER VI. 47
GLOSSARY OF RABBINICAL WORDS 54

PREFACE

THIS metaphysical essay, called "Sepher Yezirah," (book on creation, or cosmogony,) which I have endeavored to render into English, with explanatory notes, is considered by all modem literati as the first philosophical book that ever was written in the Hebrew language. But the time of its composition and the name of its author have not yet been ascertained, despite of the most elaborate researches of renowned archaeologists. Some maintain that this essay is mentioned in the Talmud treatise Sanhedrin, p. 66 b. and ibid. 67 b. which passage is according to the commentary of Rashi, to treatise Erubin, p. 63 a., a reliable historical notice. Hence this book was known already in the second or at the beginning of the third century of the Christian Era. The historian, Dr. Graetz, tries to show very ingeniously in his work, entitled "Gnosticism," p. 104 and 110, that it was written in the early centuries of the Christian Church, especially when the ideas and views of the Gnostics were in vogue. This opinion, however, he afterwards revoked. (See Dr. Graetz's "History of the Jews," Vol. V, p. 315 in a note.)

Dr. Zunz, the Nestor of the Jewish Rabbis in Europe, maintains that we have to look for the genesis of the book "Yezirah" in the Geonic period, (700-1000), and that it was consequently composed in a post-talmudical time. But if so, it is very strange that Saadjah Gaon, who lived in the tenth, and Judah Halevi, who lived in the twelfth century, represented the book "Yezirah" as a very ancient work. Therefore it seems to me, that Dr. Graetz had no sufficient cause to repudiate his assertion concerning the age of this book; because all the difficulties which he himself and others raised against his supposition, fall to the ground, when we consider that the most ancient works, holy as well as profane, had one and the same fate, namely, that from age to age more or less interpolations were made by copyists and commentators. Compare also Prof. Tenneman's "Grundriss der Geschichte der Philosophie," improved by Prof. Wendt, p. 207.

Tradition, which ascribes the authorship of this book to the patriarch Abraham, is fabulous, as can be proved by many reasons; but the idea that Rabbi Akiba, who lived about the beginning of the second century, composed the book "Yezirah," is very likely possible. Be this as it may, it is worth while to know the extravagant hypotheses which ancient Jewish philosophers and theologians framed as soon as they began to contemplate and to reason, endeavoring to combine oriental and Greek theories. Although there is an exuberance of weeds, we will find, nevertheless, many germs of truisms, which are of the greatest importance. A Christian theologian, Johann Friedrich von Meyer D. D., remarked very truly in his German preface to the book "Yezirah," published in Leipzig, 1830: "This book is for two reasons highly important: in the first place, that the real Cabala, or mystical doctrine of the Jews, which must be carefully distinguished from its excrescences, is in close connection and perfect accord with the Old and New Testaments; and in the second place, that the knowledge of it is of great importance to the philosophical inquirers, and can not be put aside. Like a cloud permeated by beams of light which makes one infer that there is more light behind it, so do the contents of this book, enveloped in obscurity, abound in coruscations of thought, reveal to the mind that there is a still more effulgent light lurking somewhere, and thus inviting us to a further contemplation and investigation, and at the same time demonstrating the danger of a superficial investigation, which is so prevalent in modem times, rejecting that which can not be understood at first sight."

I shall now try to give a sketch of the system as it is displayed in the book "Yezirah," which forms a link in the chain of the ancient theoretical speculations of philosophers, who were striving to ascertain the truth mainly by reasoning a-priori, and who imagined that it is thus possible to permeate all the secrets of nature. It teaches that a first cause, eternal, all-wise, almighty and holy, is the origin and the centre of the whole universe, from whom gradually all beings emanated. Thought, speech and action are an inseparable unity in the divine being; God made or created, is metaphorically expressed by the word: writing. The Hebrew language and its characters correspond mostly with the things they designate, and thus holy thoughts, Hebrew language and its reduction to writing, form a unity which produce a creative effect.[1]

The self-existing first cause called the creation into existence by quantity and quality; the former represented by ten numbers, (Sephiroth,) the latter by twenty-two letters, which form together thirty-two ways of the divine wisdom. Three of the twenty-two letters, namely, Aleph, Mem, Sheen, are the mothers, or the first elements, from which came forth the primitive matter of the world: air, water and fire, that have their parallel in man, (male and female): breast, body and head, and

---

[1] Thus for instance, they imagined that the name of Jehovah, יהו, is by reversing the alphabet; מצפע (mzpz); mem signifies the letter jod, zaddi, the letter he, and pe, the letter wav. These unmeaning sounds, they said, have magic power. Some maintained that the Hebrew language consists of twenty-two consonants, because being the complex of all beings, its number is equal to the most perfect figure, namely, of the periphery, as it is well known that the diameter is always to the periphery as seven to twenty-two.

in the year: moisture, cold and heat. The other seven double and twelve[1] simple letters are then represented as stamina, from which other spheres or media of existence emanated.

Man is a microcosm, as the neck separates rationality from vitality, so does diaphragm the vitality from the vegetativeness. God stands in close connection with the Universe, and just so is Tali connected with the world, that is, an invisible, celestial or universal axis carries the whole fabric. In the year by the sphere, in man by the heart, and thus is the ruling spirit of God everywhere. Notwithstanding the decay of the individual, the genus is produced by the antithesis of man and wife.

Hebrew commentaries on the book "Yezirah" were composed by: first, Saadjah Gaon, of Fajum in Egypt, (892-942); second, Rabbi Abraham ben Dior Halevi; third, Rabbi Moses ben Nachman; fourth, Elieser of Germisa; fifth, Moses Botarel; sixth, Rabbi Eliah Wilna: The book "Yezirah," together with all these commentaries, was published in 1860, in the city of Lemberg. But although the commentator Saadjah was a sober minded scholar in a superstitious age, a good Hebrew grammarian, a renowned theologian and a good translator of the Hebrew Pentateuch, Isaiah and Job into the Arabian language, his ideas and views were, nevertheless, very often much benighted. See his comments on Yez. Chap. I, etc., etc.; his notes on "Yezirah" Chap. III, 2, prove undoubtedly that he had no knowledge whatever of natural science, and therefore his annotations on

---

[1] It was frequently observed by Jewish and Christian theologians, that the Marcosianio Gnostic system, as well as that of the Clementinians of the second century, contain many analogies and parallels with the book "Yezirah." Marcus divides the Greek alphabet into three parts, namely: nine mute consonants ἄφωνα, eight half vowels ἡμιφωνα, and seven vowels φωνηεντα, in order to give a clear idea of the peculiar constitution of his "Aeons." (Irenaeus Haer, I, 16.)

the book "Yezirah" are of little or no use at all. All the other commentaries mentioned above, together with all quotations of other expounders of the same book, contain nothing but a medley of arbitrary, mystical explanations and sophistical distortions of scriptural verses, astrological notions, oriental superstitions, a metaphysical jargon, a poor knowledge of physics and not a correct elucidation of the ancient book; they drew mostly from their own imagination, and credited the author of "Yezirah" with saying very strange things which he never thought of. I must not omit to mention two other Hebrew commentaries, one by Judah Halevi, and the other by Ebn Ezra, who lived in the first part of the twelfth century. They succeeded in explaining the book "Yezirah" in a sound scientific manner, but failed in making themselves generally understood, on account of the superstitious age in which they lived, and the tenacity with which the people in that period adhered to the marvelous and supernatural; they found, therefore, but few followers, and the 'book "Yezirah" remained to the public an enigma and an ancient curiosity, giving rise to a system of metaphysical delirium, called Cabala.

Translations of the book "Yezirah" and comments thereon by learned Christian authors are: first, a translation of the book "Yezirah" with explanatory notes in the Latin language, by Wilhelm Postellus, Paris, France, 1552; second, another Latin version is contained in Jo. Pistorii artis cabalistical scriptorum, Tom I, p. 869, sqq., differing from that of Postellus. Some are of the opinion that John Reuchlin, while others maintain that Paul Riccius was the author of it. (See Wolfii Biblioth. Hebr. Tom., I, Chap. 1.) Third, Rittangel published the book "Yezirah," 1642, at Amsterdam, entitled: "Liber Yezirah qui Abrahamo patriarchae adscribitur, una cum commentario Rabbi Abraham F. D. (filii Dior) super 32 Semitis Sapientiae, a quibus liber Yezirah incipit. Translatus et notis illustrates, a Joanne Stephano Rittangelio, ling. Orient. in Elect. Acad. Regiomontana Prof. extraord. Amstelodami ap. Jo. and Jodoc. Janssonios," 1642, in quarto; fourth, Johann Friedrich von Mayer, D. D., published the book "Yezirah" in Hebrew with a translation and explanatory notes in the German language, Leipzig, 1830.

All these translations are out of print and are rarely found even in well regulated libraries. I was so fortunate as to obtain a copy of Dr. Mayer's edition of the book "Yezirah." He states in the preface to it, that he had a copy of Postellus' translation in manuscript as well as some others, and compared them. The explanatory notes given by this author are, nevertheless, insufficient and sometimes very incorrect. The present translation is, as far as I could ascertain, the first that was ever published in the English language. Again, I have to add that I have not only endeavored to correct a great many mistakes and erroneous ideas of my predecessors, but I have also endeavored to give more complete annotations. I therefore hope that the candid reader will consider the great difficulties I had to overcome in this still unbeaten way of the ancient Jewish spiritual region, and will receive with indulgence this new contribution to archaeological knowledge.

DR. ISIDOR KALISCH

CHAPTER I.

SECTION 1

YAH,[1] the Lord of hosts, the living God, King of the Universe, Omnipotent, All-Kind and Merciful, Supreme and Extolled, who is Eternal, Sublime and Most-Holy, ordained (formed) and created the Universe in thirty-two [2] mysterious paths [3] of wisdom by three [4] Sepharim, namely: 1)

---

[1] Our author maintains that there is a first intelligent, self-existing, almighty, eternal ruling cause of all things, and that an everlasting entity produced nonentities by a progression of effects. The divine knowledge, he adds, differs from the human knowledge in such a degree, that it gives existence to all that is. צבאות ח״ יח חקק is a talmudical expression. (See Treatise Bava Bathra p. 93.) It seems to me, that the author not only wanted to contradict Plato's assertion that the Supreme Being had need of a plan, like the human architect, to conduct the great design, when he made the fabric of the Universe, but also the common belief that God reasons and acts by ideas like a human being. As the prophet Isaiah exclaimed: "Behold! God has no ideas like you, and his ways of acting are not like yours." (Isaiah 55, 8-9.)

[2] The number thirty-two is not only the fifth power of two, and the sum of ten units and twenty-two letters, but is also the sum of the first and last letter of the Hebrew Pentateuch, namely: ב 2 and 30, equal thirty-two. (See Kusari p. 343, translated into German by Dr. David Cassel.)

[3] Paths denote powers, effects, kinds, forms, degrees or stages.

[4] These Sepharim or three words of similar expression signify: first, number, calculation or idea; second, the word; third, the writing of the *word. The idea, word and writing (of the word), are signs to man for a thing, and is not the thing itself, to the Creator, however, idea, word

S'for סְפָר; 2) Sippur סִפּוּר; and 3) Sapher סֵפֶר which are in Him one and the same. They consist of a decade out of nothing [1] and of twenty-two fundamental letters. He divided the twenty-two consonants into three divisions: 1) three א מות mothers, fundamental letters or first elements; 2) seven double; and 3) twelve simple consonants.

יצירה ספר.

ראשון פרק.

א. משנה

הָקַק חָכְמָה פְּלִיאוֹת נְתִיבוֹת וּשְׁתַּיִם בִּשְׁלֹשִׁים

שַׁדַּי אֵל עוֹלָם וּמֶלֶךְ הַיִּים אֱ לֹהִים צְבָאוֹת יְהֹוָה יָהּ

שְׁמוֹ וְקָדוֹשׁ מָרוֹם עַד שׁוֹכֵן וְנִשָּׂא רָם וְחַנּוּן רַחוּם

וְסִפּוּר בְּסֵפָר* סְפָרִים בִּשְׁלֹשָׁה עוֹלָמוֹ אֶת וּבָרָא

וּשְׁתַּיִם וְעֶשְׂרִים בְּלִימָה סְפִירוֹת עֶשֶׂר וְסֵפֶר:

וּשְׁתֵּים כְּפוּלוֹת וְשֶׁבַע אִמּוֹת שָׁלֹשׁ יְסוֹד: אוֹתִיּוֹת

---

and writing (of the word) are the thing itself, or as some ancient Rabbis remarked: "בהק״ב״ה׳ אחד דבו הרא הכל ימעשה דביר מחשבה, Idea, word and work are one and the same to God." There is an ideal world in the divine intellect, according to which this sensible world was made. The difference between the human and divine manner of thinking admits no comparison.

[1] This means to say, that there has not been any matter or hyle existing from all eternity, containing different kinds of primitive atoms or molecules etc., as the Greek philosopher, Anaxagoras, taught, but that all things are the gradual emanations of one everlasting being. This idea is then symbolically explained in the next paragraph.

פְּשׁוּטוֹת: עֲשָׂרָה

וְסִפּוּר: וְסוֹפֵר בְּסֵפֶר. נ"א (*

SECTION 2

The decade [1] out of nothing is analogous to that of the ten fingers (and toes) of the human body, five parallel to five, and in the centre of which is the covenant with the only One, by the word of the tongue and the rite of Abraham.

ב. משנה

אֶצְבָּעוֹת עֶשֶׂר כְּמִסְפָּר בְּלִימָה סְפִירוֹת עֶשֶׂר

בְּאֶמְצַע מְכֻוֶּנֶת יָחִיד וּבְרִית חָמֵשׁ כְּנֶגֶד הָמֵשׁ

הַמָּעוֹר: וּבְמִלַּת הַלָּשׁוֹן בְּמִלַּת

---

[1] The design of the author is evidently to deduce the proof of the decade from the phenomena in the nature of man, who is generally considered the crown or the final cause of the terrestrial creation, and upon whom God vouchsafed two most precious gifts, namely: the articulated word, and the religious element (spiritual purity). This passage is explained by Isaac Satanow in his Hebrew Dictionary entitled Sephath Emeth, p. 44, b:

המוליד ואבר השכלים לתולדות סופר עט הוא הלשין דחנה
האדם את לקיים עולם ברית הוא אחד ובל החמריים לתולדות
כדאיתיה האי וצורתו חמרו צלעותיו שתי על נצחרת לפליטה
בצורתו וזה בחמרו זה כדאיתיה והאי.

The tongue is, as it were, the descriptive pen of all the spiritual issues, and the genital parts are the originators of the corporeal substances. Every one of them is an eternal covenant in order to preserve the human race for ever, according to its two-fold being: body and spirit. Each working after its own way, physically and spiritually.

SECTION 3

Ten are the numbers out of nothing, and not the number nine, ten and not eleven. Comprehend this great wisdom, understand this [1] knowledge, inquire into it and ponder on it, render it evident and lead [2] the Creator back to His throne again.

.ג משנה

וְ לֹא עֶשֶׂר תֵּשַׁע וְ לֹא עֶשֶׂר בְּלִימָה סְפִירוֹת עֶשֶׂר

בָּהוֹן בְּבִינָה נְחָכַם בְּחָכְמָה הָבֵן עֶשְׂרֵה אַחַת

יוֹצֵר וְהוֹשֵׁב וְהוֹשֵׁב בּוֹרְיוֹ עַל דָּבָר וְהַעֲמֵד מֵהֶם זְחָקוֹר בָּהֶם

מְכוֹנוֹ:-עַל

SECTION 4

The decade out of nothing has the following ten infinitudes:

    1) The beginning [3] infinite.   6) The depth infinite.

---

[1] Like Pythagoras, who taught that the digits inclusive number ten which are typified in Tetraktys, (Τετρακτὺς) namely: 1 plus 2 plus 3 plus 4 equal 10, and which comprise the whole arithmetical system of nature, etc. Our author endeavors to show the gradual emanation of all things from God, which were completely finished in ten spheres.

[2] My Hebrew reading is: על יוצר והושב There are various readings; therefore Postellus rendered it: "restitue figmentum in locum suum;" Rittangel, "restitue formatorem in throno suo;" Pistorius, "fac sedere creatorem in throno suo." The author seems to ridicule here the Gnosticians who maintained that Demiurg was the creator of man and the sensual world.

[3] In God is the beginning and he is the boundary of the Universe. Compare also the Talmud treatise Chagigah p. 12.

2) " end "	7) " East "
3) " good "	8) " West "
4) " evil [1] "	9) " North "
5) " height "	10) " South "

and the only Lord God, the faithful King, rules over all from His holy habitation for ever and ever.

ד. משנה

לָהֶם שֶׁאֵין עֶשֶׂר עָשָׂר מִדָּתָן בְּלִימָה סְפִירוֹת עֶשֶׂר

וְעוֹמֶק טוֹב עוֹמֶק אַחֲרִית וְעוֹמֶק רֵאשִׁית עוֹמֶק סוֹף

וְעוֹמֶק מִזְרָח עוֹמֶק תַּחַת וְעוֹמֶק רוֹם עוֹמֶק רָע

מֶלֶךְ אֵל יָחִיד אָדוֹן דָּרוֹם וְעוֹמֶק צָפוֹן עוֹמֶק מַעֲרָב

עַד: עֲדֵי עַד קָדְשׁוֹ מִמְּעוֹן בְּכֻלָּם מוֹשֵׁל נֶאֱמָן

SECTION 5

The appearance of the ten spheres out of nothing is like a flash of lightning, being without an end, His word is in them, when they go and return; they run by His order like a whirlwind and humble themselves before His throne.

---

[1] Here is contradicted the system of ditheism, consisting of an eternal God, the Author of all good and of "Hyle" or "Satan," the co-eternal and co-equal principle of evil, maintaining that an all-perfect God alone is the author of all good and evil, and has in his infinite wisdom so wonderfully contrived the nature of things, that physical and moral evil may produce good, and hence contribute to carry out the great design of the Supreme Being. Compare also Chap. 6 §5.

ה. משנה

הַבָּנֵק כְּמַרְאֵה צְפִיָּתָן בְּלִימָה סְפִירוֹת עֶשֶׂר

וָשׁוֹב בְּרָצוֹא בָּהֶן דְּבָרוֹ קֵץ לָהֶן אֵין וְתִכְלִיתָן

מִשְׁתַּחֲוִים: הֵם כִּסְאוֹ וְלִפְנֵי יִרְדּוֹפוּ כְּסוּפָה וּלְמַאֲמָרוֹ

SECTION 6

The decade of existence out of nothing has its end linked to its beginning and its beginning linked to its end, just as the flame is wedded to the live coal; because the Lord is one and there is not a second one, and before one what wilt thou count? [1]

ו. משנה

וּתְחִלָּתָן בְּתַחְלָתָן סוֹפָן נָעוּץ בְּלִימָה סְפִירוֹת עֶשֶׂר

וְאֵין יָחִיד שֶׁאָדוֹן בְּגַחֶלֶת *קְשׁוּרָה כְּשַׁלְהֶבֶת בְּמוֹפָן

סוֹפֵר: אַתָּה מַה אֶחָד וְלִפְנֵי שֵׁנִי לוֹ

יְצִירָה סֵפֶר בַּעַל בָּתַב וו"ל הַקְמִיצָה בְּסֵפֶר כָּתַב ז"ל נָאוֹן הָא" רַבֵּינוּ (*
בְּנֶהֱלֶת: שׁוֹרָה בְּשַׁלְהֶבֶת

SECTION 7

Concerning the number ten of the spheres of existence out of nothing keep thy tongue from speaking and thy mind from pondering on it, and if thy mouth urges thee to speak, and thy heart to think about it, return! as it reads: "And the living

---

[1] As the infinite series of numbers starts from one unit, so was the whole Universe formed a unity, that centres in the Godhead.

creatures ran and returned," (Ezekiel 1,14.) and upon this [1] was the covenant made.

ז. משנה

וְלִבְּךָ מִלְדַבֵּר פִּיךָ בְּלוֹם בְּלִימָה סְפִירוֹת עֶשֶׂר

שׁוּב לְהַרְהֵר לְדַבֵּר פִּיךָ רָץ וְאִם מִלְהַרְהֵר

דָבָר וְאֶל וָשׁוּב רָצוֹא וְהַחַיּוֹת נֶאֱמַר שֶׁלְּכָךְ לַמָּקוֹם

בְּרִית: נִכְרַת זֶה

SECTION 8

The following are the ten categories of existence out of nothing:

1) The spirit of the living God, praised and glorified be the name of Him who lives to all eternity. The articulate word of creative power, the spirit and the word are what we call the holy spirit is

2) Air emanated from the spirit by which He formed and established twenty-two consonants, stamina. Three of them, however, are fundamental letters, or mothers, seven double and twelve simple consonants; hence the spirit is the first one.

---

[1] The meaning is, that as the living creatures which the prophet saw in his vision were stricken with such an awe, that they could not go any further to see the divine glory, and had to return, so is the decade an eternal secret to us and we are not permitted to understand it. We find this very idea in the Pythagorean system. The disciples of Pythagoras looked upon the decade as a holy number, and swore by it and by the Tetraktys which contain the number ten,

3) Primitive water emanated from the air. He formed and established by it Bohu [1] (water, stones) mud and loam, made them like a bed, put them up like a wall, and surrounded them as with a rampart, put coldness upon them and they became dust, as it reads: "He says to the snow (coldness) be thou earth." (Job 37, 6.)

4) Fire or ether emanated from the water. He established by it the throne of glory, the Seraphim and Ophanim, the holy living creatures and the angels, and of these three He formed His habitation, as it reads: "Who made His angels spirits, His ministers a flaming fire." (Psalm 104, 4.) He selected three consonants from the simple ones which are in the hidden secret of three mothers or first elements: א"מ"ש, air, water and ether

---

[1] I adopted here the reading of Judah Halevi, namely:
בהו וחצב חקק
וגו וטיט רפש בהו,
with the exception of the word תהו because it is obvious from "Yezirah," Chap. II, that the author signifies by the word "Tohu," nothing, and not something, as Judah Halevi erroneously thought. Moses Butarel and others tell us that they had before them a correct copy of "Sepher Yezirah," where it reads:
אבנים אלו בהו וכו' ירוק קו זה תהו
מפולמות:
The same passage is mentioned in the Talmud treatise Chagigah, p. 12, a, with the addition of
יוצאין שמהן בתהום המשוקעות
מים.
The word המפולמות is translated by Rashi, *moist*. Some say it is a compound word of מות מפול; others of אלמוני פלוני, etc. But the word is not of Semitic origin; it is, according to my opinion, borrowed from the Greek as the word סימן, etc., Πλημη *flood*. מפלמות אבנים flood-stones. The same word is used treatise Beza, p. 24, b, המפולמין דגים fish that are caught from out of the flood.

or fire. He sealed them with spirit and fastened them to His great name and sealed with it six dimensions. [1]

ח. משנה

הַיָּם אֱלֹהִים רוּחַ אַחַת בְּלִימָה סְפִירוֹת עֶשֶׂר

וְרוּחַ קוֹל הָעוֹלָמִים חַי שֶׁל שְׁמוֹ וּמְבוֹרָךְ בָּרוּךְ

חָקַק מֵרוּחַ רוּחַ שְׁתַּיִם הַקּוֹדֶשׁ: רוּחַ וְהוּא וְדִבּוּר

אִמּוֹת שָׁלֹשׁ יְסוֹד אוֹתִיּוֹת וּשְׁתַּיִם עֶשְׂרִים בָּהּ וְחָצַב

אַחַת וְרוּחַ פְּשׁוּטוֹת עֶשְׂרֵה וּשְׁתֵּים בְּפוּלוֹת וְשֶׁבַע

עֶשְׂרִים) בָּהֶן וְחָצַב חָקַק מֵרוּחַ מַיִם שָׁלֹשׁ מֵהֶן:

כְּמִין חֲקָקָן יָטִיט רֶפֶשׁ נ בֹהוּ תֹהוּ (אוֹתִיּוֹת וּשְׁתַּיִם

מַעֲזִיבָה כְּמִין **סִכְּכֵם חוֹמָה כְּמִין *הִצִּיבָן עֲרוּגָה

לַשֶּׁלֶג כִּי שֶׁנֶּאֱמַר עָפָר וְנַעֲשָׂה שֶׁלֶג עֲלֵיהֶם וַיִּצֹק)

בָּהּ וְחָצַב הָקַק מִמַּיִם אֵשׁ אַרְבַּע: (אֶרֶץ הֶרָא יֹאמַר

וּמַלְאֲכֵי הַקּוֹדֶשׁ וְהָיוּת? וְאוֹפַנִּים שְׂרָפִים הַכָּהוֹד כִּסֵּא

עוֹשֶׂה שֶׁנֶּאֱמַר מְעוֹנוֹ יָסַד וּמְשַׁלֶּשְׁתָּן חַשְׁרַת

שְׁלֹשָׁה בֵּירֵר לוֹהֵט אֵשׁ מְשָׁרְתָיו רוּחוֹת מַלְאָכָיו

***אֱ״מֵ״ש אִמּוֹת שָׁלֹשׁ בְּסוֹד הַפְּשׁוּטוֹת מִן אוֹתִיּוֹת

---

[1] According to the author, the space and six dimensions emanated from the ether.

קְצָווֹת: שֵׁשׁ בָּהֶם וְהָתַם הַגָּדוֹל בִּשְׁמוֹ וְקָבְעָם

הַצְּבָן: אחרינא: נוסחא (*)

סִיבְבָן: נ"א (**)

שָׁלֹשׁ: בְּעַד ווֹה הָתַם הוֹסִיף: יֵשׁ (***)

5) He sealed [1] the height and turned towards above, and sealed it with יהו

6) He sealed the depth, turned towards below and sealed it with היו

7) He sealed the east and turned forward, and sealed it with ויה

8) He Sealed the west and turned backward, and sealed it with והי

9) He sealed the south and turned to the right and sealed it with יוה

---

[1] Judah Halevi in his book entitled "Kusari," p. 456, illustrates it thus: The Creator is one, and the space has in the figurative expression six dimensions. The book "Yezirah," having ascribed to the Creator some names in the spiritual language, chooses now in the human language the finest sounds which are, as it were, the spirits of the other sounds, namely: "הוי" and says, that when the divine will was expressed by such a sublime name, it became that which the Exalted by praise wished to call forth according to the combination of "הוי." Hence it follows, that the material world was created in such a way and manner which corresponds with the material, namely, by the sublime spiritual name, which corresponds with the material name, הוי, יוה, יהו, והי, ויה, היו, and out of each of them became one dimension of the world, the sphere.

10) He sealed the north and turned to the left and sealed it with הוי

ביהו וְחֲתָמוֹ לְמַעְלָה וּפָנָה רוּם חָתַם הָמֵשׁ

בהיו וְחֲתָמוֹ לְמַטָּה וּפָנָה תַּחַת חָתַם שֵׁשׁ

בויה וְחֲתָמוֹ לְפָנָיו וּפָנָה מִזְרָח חָתַם שֶׁבַע

בוהי וְחֲתָמוֹ לְאַחֲרָיו וּפָנָה מַעֲרָב חָתַם שְׁמוֹנָה

ביוה וְחֲתָמוֹ לִימִינוֹ וּפָנָה דָּרוֹם חָתַם תֵּ אֵע

בהוי וְחֲתָמוֹ לִשְׂ מֹאלוֹ וּפָנָה צָפוֹן חָתַם אֲשֶׁר

SECTION 9

These are the ten spheres of existence out of nothing. From the spirit of the living God emanated air, from the air, water, from the water, fire or ether, from the ether, the height and the depth, the East and West, the North and South.

ט. משנה

אֱלֹהִים רִיחַ אַחַת בְּלִימָה סְפִירוֹת עֶשֶׂר אֵלּוּ

וְתַחַת רוּם מִמַּיִם אֵשׁ מֵרוּחַ מַיִם מֵרוּחַ רוּחַ חַיִּים

וְדָרוֹם: צָפוֹן וּמַעֲרָב מִזְרָח

CHAPTER II.

SECTION 1

THERE are twenty-two letters, stamina. Three of them, however, are the first elements, fundamentals or mothers, seven double and twelve simple consonants. The three fundamental letters א"מ"ש have as their basis the balance. In one scale [1] is the merit and in the other criminality, which are placed in equilibrium by the tongue. The three fundamental letters א"מ"ש signify, as מ is mute like the water and ש hissing like the fire, there is א among them, a breath of air which reconciles them.

פרק שני.

משנה א.

וְשֶׁבַע אִמּוֹת שָׁלשׁ יְסוֹד אוֹתִיּוֹת וּשְׁתַּיִם עֶשְׂרִים

אֶ"מֶ"ש אִמּוֹת שָׁלשׁ פְּשׁוּטוֹת עֶשְׂרֵה וּשְׁתֵּים כְּפוּלוֹת

בֵּנְתַיִם מַכְרִיעַ חָק וְלָשׁוֹן חוֹבָה וְכַף זְכוּת כַּף יְסוֹדָן

אֲוִיר א׳ שׁוֹרֶקֶת שׁ׳ דּוֹמֶמֶת מ׳ אֶ"מֶ"ש אִמּוֹת שָׁלשׁ

בֵּנְתַיִם: מַכְרִיעַ רוּחַ

---

[1] The author shows here by the symbol of a scale and the phonetic character of the fundamental letters א"מ"ש, that the opposite forces and the struggle which prevail in the smallest as well as in the largest circles of creation are appeased and calmed.

SECTION 2

The twenty-two letters which form the stamina after having been appointed and established by God, He combined, weighed and changed them, and formed by them all beings which are in existence, and all those which will be formed in all time to come.

ב. מִשְׁנָה

צְרָפָן חֲצָבָן חֲקָקָן יְסוֹד אוֹתִיּוֹת וּשְׁתַּיִם עֶשְׂרִים

כָּל וְאֶת הַיְצוּר כָּל אֶת בָּהֶם וְצָר וְהֵמִירָן שְׁקָלָן

לָצוּר: הֶעָתִיד

SECTION 3

He established twenty-two letters, stamina, by the voice, formed by the breath of air and fixed them on five places in the human mouth, namely: 1) gutturals, א ה ח ע (2) palatals, ג י כ ק (3) linguals, ד ט ל נ ת (4) dentals, ז ש ס ר ץ (5) labials, ב ו מ ף

ג. מִשְׁנָה

חֲצָבָן בְּקוֹל חֲקָקָן יְמוֹד אוֹתִיּוֹת וּשְׁתַּיִם עֶשְׂרִים

אַהָחַ"ע אוֹתִיּוֹת מְקוֹמוֹת בַּחֲמִשָּׁה בַּפֶּה קְבָעָן בְּרוּחַ

בַּשִּׁנַּיִם זְשַׂסְרַ"ץ בַּלָּשׁוֹן רַטְלְנָ"ת בַּחֵיךְ גִּיכַ"ק בַּגָּרוֹן

בַּשְּׂפָתַיִם: בּוּמַ"ף

SECTION 4

He fixed the twenty-two letters, stamina, on the sphere like a wall with two hundred and thirty-one gates,[1] and turned the spheres forward and backward. For an illustration may serve the three letters, ג נ ע. There is nothing better than joy, and nothing worse than sorrow or plague is.[2]

ד. משנה

בְּמִין בְּגַלְגַּל קָבְאָן יְסוֹד אוֹתִיּוֹת וּשְׁתַּיִם עֶשְׂרִים

וְאָחוֹר פָּנִים הַגַּלְגַּלִים וְחוֹוֹר שְׁעָרִים בְּרל'א חוֹמָה

בְּרָעָה וְאֵין מִ עֹנֶג לְמַעְלָה בְּטוֹבָה אֵין לְרָבָר וְסִימָן

מִנֶּגַע: לְמַטָּה

SECTION 5

But how was it done? He combined,[3] weighed and changed: the א with all the other letters in succession, and all the others again with א; ב with all, and all again with ב; and so the whole series of letters.[4] Hence it follows that there are two hundred

---

[1] Meaning outlets, outgates of the creative power, formations.
[2] The word ענג signifies joy, and when transposed, forming the word נגע it signifies just the contrary, trouble, plague. He means to say, that the letters of the words ענג and נגע are the same, but they signify nevertheless, opposite ideas on account of transposition. Just as the sphere remains the same during the rotation on its axis in its setting and in its rising; yet it appears to us as if it had undergone a great change on account of its different position.
[3] My reading is וְחֲמִינָן שָׁקְלָן עָרְפָן.
[4] The combination of the twenty-two letters without permutation is represented in the following table:

and thirty-one [1] formations, and that every creature and every word emanated from one names. [2]

ח. מִשְׁנָה.

א עִם וְכֻלָּן כֻּלָּן עִם א וְהֶמִירָן שְׁקָלָן צְרָפָן בְּיָצַד

וְנִמְצָאוֹת חֲלִילָה נְחוֹרוֹת ב עִם וְכֻלָּן כֻּלָּן עִם ב

אב	אג	אד	אה	או	אז	אח	אט	אי	אכ	אל	אם	אן	אס	אע	אף	אצ	אק	אר	אש	את
בג	בד	בה	בו	בז	בח	בט	בי	בכ	בל	בם	בן	בס	בע	בף	בץ	בק	בר	בש	בת	
גד	גה	גו	גז	גח	גט	גי	גכ	גל	גם	גן	גס	גע	גף	גץ	גק	גר	גש	גת		
דה	דו	דז	דח	דט	די	דכ	דל	דם	דן	דס	דע	דף	דץ	דק	דר	דש	דת			
הו	הז	הח	הט	הי	הכ	הל	הם	הן	הס	הע	הף	הץ	הק	הר	הש	הת				
וז	וח	וט	וי	וכ	ול	ום	ון	וס	וע	וף	וץ	וק	ור	וש	ות					
זח	זט	זי	זכ	זל	זם	זן	זס	זע	זף	זץ	זק	זר	זש	זת						
חט	חי	חכ	חל	חם	חן	חס	חע	חף	חץ	חק	חר	חש	חת							
טי	טכ	טל	טם	טן	טס	טע	טף	טץ	טק	טר	טש	טת								
יכ	יל	ים	ין	יס	יע	יף	יץ	יק	יר	יש	ית									
כל	כם	כן	כס	כע	כף	כץ	כק	כר	כש	כת										
לם	לן	לס	לע	לף	לץ	לק	לר	לש	לת											
מן	מס	מע	מף	מץ	מק	מר	מש	מת												
נס	נע	נף	נץ	נק	נר	נש	נת													
סע	סף	סץ	סק	סר	סש	סת														
עף	עץ	עק	ער	עש	עת															
פץ	פק	פר	פש	פת																
צק	צר	צש	צת																	
קר	קש	קת																		
רש	רת																			
שת																				

[1] The number of combinations of twenty-two letters two and two without any permutation is according to the mathematical formula

$$n \cdot \frac{n-1}{2} = 22 - 1 \times \frac{22}{2} = 231.$$

[2] The ancient philosophers maintained that if God is the first cause, and He is necessarily, He, the immediate effect of Him, as an absolute unity, can only be again a unity. Hence from a being that is in every respect a unique being, there can only emanate one being; because would two essentially and truly different things issue conjointly from one being, they can only proceed from two different things of substance, that would consequently admit a division that is inconceivable. They then put the question, how came so many various beings into existence? Our author is therefore endeavoring to show that the whole universe emanated gradually from the spirit of the one living God.

יוֹצֵא הַדִּבּוּר וְכָל הַיְצוּר כָּל וְנִמְצָא שְׁעָרִים בָּרל"א

אֶחָד: *מִשֵּׁם

בְּשֵׁם: נ"א (*

SECTION 6

He created a reality out of nothing, called the nonentity into existence and hewed, as it were, colossal pillars from intangible air. This has been shown by the example of combining the letter א with all the other letters, and all the other letters with Aleph (א). He [1] predetermined, and by speaking created every creature and every word by one name. For an illustration may serve the twenty-two elementary substances by the primitive substance of Aleph [2] (א).

ו. משנה

וְחָצַב יֶשְׁנוֹ אֵינוֹ אֶת וְעָשָׂה מ תֹּהוּ מִתֹּשׁ מַמָּשׁ יָצָר

---

[1] The reading of Von Jo. Meyer and others is as follows:
מתוחו יצר
נתפס שאינו מאויר גדולים עמודים והצב ישנו אינו ועשח ממש
אחר בשם הדברים כל ואת היצור כל עושח ומימר צופה סימן ויח
אחג: דגוף מניינם ושתים עשרים לדבר וסימן

My reading according to a manuscript of Rabbi Isaac Luria, which I have preferred to all others, is thus:
גדולים עמודים וחצב ישנו אינו את ועשה מתוהו ממש יצר
צופה א עם וכולן כולן עם א אות סימן וזח נתפס שאינו מאדיר
לדבר וסימן אחד שם חדבור כל ואת היצור כל ועשה ומימר
א: בגוף חפצים ושתים עשרום

[2] It has been already mentioned above Chap. i, §1, that God, his idea and his word are a unity; hence the author signifies by the letter Aleph the air from which emanated the creative speech, etc.

אוֹת סִימָן וָוֶה נִתְפָּם שֶׁאֵינוֹ מֵאִיר גְּדוֹלִים עַמּוּדִים

כָּל אֶת וְעָשָׂה וּמֵימַר צוֹפֶה א עִם נָכֵלָן כֻּלָּן עִם א

לְדָבָר וְסִימָן אֶחָד שֵׁם הַדִּבּוּר כָּל וְאֶת הַיְצוּר

א: בְּגוּף חֲפָצִים וּשְׁתַּיִם עֶשְׂרִים

CHAPTER III.

SECTION 1

THE three first elements, א"מ"ש are typified by a balance, in one scale the merit and in the other the criminality, which are placed in equilibrium by the tongue. These three mothers, א"מ"ש are a great, wonderful and unknown mystery, and are sealed by six [1] rings, or elementary circles, namely: air, water and fire emanated from them, which gave birth to progenitors, and these progenitors gave birth again to some offspring.

פרק שלישי.

א. משנה

שָׁלֹשׁ אִמּוֹת אֶ"מֶ"ש יְסוֹדָן כַּף זְכוּת וְכַף חוֹבָה

סוֹד אֶ"מֶ"ש אִמּוֹת שָׁלֹשׁ בְּנְתַיִם מַכְרִיעַ חַק וְלָשׁוֹן

*וְיָצְאוּ טַבָּעוֹת בְּשֵׁשׁ וְחָתוּם וּמְכוּסָה מוּפְלָא גָּדוֹל

וּמְאָכוֹת אָבוֹת נוֹלְדוּ וּמֵהֶם וְאֵשׁ וּמַיִם אַוִּיר מֵהֶם

תּוֹלְדוֹת:

---

[1] Here is meant: ethereal air, ethereal water, ethereal fire, the macrocosm, the courses of time and microcosm. Many offspring or derivations came from the latter three, as their progenitors, as it is explained afterwards in the chapter.

אִמּוֹת שָׁלֹשׁ וּנְקֵבָה זָכָר וּמִתְחַלְּקִים וּמַיִם אֵשׁ יוֹצְאִים וּמִמֶּנּוּ נ"א (*

הַבַל: נִבְרָע שֶׁמִּמֶּנּוּ אָבוֹת נוֹלְדוּ וּמֵהֶן יְסוֹדָן אֱ"מֶ"ש

SECTION 2

God appointed and established the three mothers, א"מ"ש combined, weighed and changed them, and formed by them three mothers א"מ"ש in the world, in the year and in man, male and female.

ב. משנה

שְׁקָלָן צְרָפָן חֲצָבָן חֲקָקָן אֱ"מֶ"ש אִמּוֹת שָׁלֹשׁ

וְשָׁלֹשׁ בָּעוֹלָם אֱ"מֶ"ש אִמּוֹת שָׁלֹשׁ בָּהֶם וְצָר וְהִירְן

בְּנֶפֶשׁ אֱ"מֶ"ש אִמּוֹת וְשָׁלֹשׁ בְּשָׁנָה אֱ"מֶ"ש אִמּוֹת

וּנְקֵבָה: זָכָר

SECTION 3

The three mothers א"מ"ש in the world are: air, water and fire. Heaven was created from fire or ether; the earth (comprising sea and land) from the elementary water; and the atmospheric air from the elementary air, or spirit, which establishes the balance among them.

ג. משנה

שָׁמַיִם וְאֵשׁ וּמַיִם אַוִּיר בָּעוֹלָם אֱ"מֶ"ש אִמּוֹת שָׁלֹשׁ

מֵרוּחַ וְאַוִּיר מִמַּיִם נִבְרֵאת וְאֶרֶץ מֵאֵשׁ נִבְרְאוּ

בְּנְתַּיִם: מַכְרִיעַ

SECTION 4

The three mothers א״מ״ש produce in the year [1]: heat, coldness [2] and moistness. Heat was created from fire, coldness from water, and moistness from air which equalizes them.

ג. משנה

חוֹם וּרְוָיָה וּקוֹר חוֹם בַּשָּׁנָה אֱ״מֶ״ש אמוֹת שָׁלֹש

מַכְרִיעַ וּרְוָיָה מִמַּיִם נִבְרָא קוֹר מֵאֵשׁ נִבְרָא

בְּנְתּוֹם:

SECTION 5

The three mothers א״מ״ש produce in man, male and female, breast, body and head. The head was created from fire, the breast from water, and the body from air, which places them in equilibrium.

ה. משנה

וּבֶטֶן רֹאשׁ נִנְקְבָה זָכָר בְּנֶפֶשׁ אֱ״מֶ״ש אמוֹת שָׁלֹש

וּגְוִיָה מִמָּרם נִבְרָא וּבֶטֶן מֵאֵשׁ נִבְרָא רֹאשׁ וּגְוִיָה

---

[1] The author endeavors to show how the creative divine word became more condensed and how a new series of productions came out of three elements.

[2] In ancient times coldness was considered to be a substance. [See Psalm 147, 17.]

בִּנְתַיִם: מַכְרִיעַ מְרוּהַ

SECTION 6

FIRST DIVISION. God let the letter. Aleph (א) predominate in primitive air, crowned [1] it, combined one with the other, [2] and formed by them the air in the world, moistness in the year, and the breast in man, male and female; in male by א"מ"ש and in female by: א"ש"ם

ו. משנה

כֶּתֶר לוֹ וְקָשַׁר בְּרוּחַ א׳ אוֹת הַמְלִיךְ. א בָּבָא

בְּשָׁנָה רְוָיָה בָּעוֹלָם אֲוִיר בָּהֶם וְצָר בָּזֶה זֶה וְצָרְפָן

בְּאָ"שָׁ"ם: וּנְקֵבָה בָּעָ"מָ"ש זָכָר בְּנֶפֶשׁ גְּוִיָּה

SECTION 7

SECOND DIVISION. He let the letter Mem (מ) predominate in primitive water, and crowned it, combined one with the other, and formed by them the earth, (including land and sea) coldness in the year, and the belly in male and female; in male by א"מ"ש [3], in female by: מ"ש"א

ז. משנה

כֶּתֶר לוֹ וְקָשַׁר בְּמַיִם מ׳ אוֹת הַמְלִיךְ. ב בָּבָא

בְּשָׁנָה וְקוֹר בָּעוֹלָם אֶרֶץ בָּהֶם נָצַר בָּזֶה זֶה וְצָרְפָן

---

[1] Id est, made it the reigning power.
[2] Namely, with the two other elements.
[3] That is to say a different combination of the elements.

בְּמַ"שׁ"א: וּנְקֵכָה *בְּאֵ"מֵ"שׁ זָכָר בְּנֶפֶשׁ וּבֶטֶן

בְּמַ"אֵ"שׁ: נ"א (*

SECTION 8

THIRD DIVISION. He let the letter Sheen (ש) predominate in primitive fire, crowned it, combined one with the other, and formed by them, heaven in the world, heat in the year, and the head of male and female. [1]

ח משנה.

כֶּתֶר לוֹ וְקִשַּׁר בָּאֵשׁ שׁ' אוֹת הַמְלִיךְ .ג בָּבָא

בְּשָׁנָה וְחוֹם בָּעוֹלָם שָׁמַיִם בָּהֶם וְצָר בָּזֶה וְצָר זֶה וְצָרְפָן

וּנְקֵבָה: זָכָר בְּנֶפֶשׁ וְ רֹאשׁ

---

[1] According to the opinion of the author, it may be arranged as follows:

	Aleph.	Mem.	Sheen.
World:	Air,	Earth, (Inclusive of Land and Sea)	Heaven or Atmosphere.
Man:	Breast,	Belly,	Head.
Year:	Moistness,	Coldness, Heat.	

CHAPTER IV.

SECTION 1

THE [1] seven double letters, with a duplicity of כפרת בגד pronunciation, aspirated and unaspirated, namely: פפ, רר, תת, בב, גג, דד, כך, serve as a model of softness and hardness, strength and weakness.

פרק רביעי.

משנה א.

בִּשְׁתֵּי מִתְנַהֲגוֹת כַּפְרַ"ת בְּגַ"ד כְּפוּלוֹת שֶׁבַע

תַּבְנִית תּ"ת ר"ר פּ"פ כּ"כ ד"ד גּ"ג ב"ב לְשׁוֹנוֹת

וְחָלָשׁ: גִּבּוֹר וְקָשָׁה רַךְ

SECTION 2

Seven [2] double letters, כפרת בגד, shall, as it were, symbolize wisdom, wealth, fruitfulness, life, dominion, peace and beauty.

---

[1] The aspirating pronunciation of ρ in the Greek, was adopted by the ancient Jews in Palestine for the Hebrew letter ר. They pronounced it partly aspirated and partly unaspirated. [See Dr. Geiger's Lehr-und Lese-buch der Mischnah, p. 22, and Dr. Graetz's Gnosticismus, p. 117.]

[2] According to the idea of our author, there emanated from the unity of God three ethereal elements: primitive air from the spirit, from the air, primitive water, and from the water, primitive fire or ether, out of which came other spheres of existence in the significant and highly

ב. מִשְׁנָה.

וְעוֹשֶׁר הַחָכְמָה יְסוֹדָן כַּפְרַ"ת בְּגַ"ד כְּפוּלוֹת שֶׁבַע

וְחֵן: שָׁלוֹם וּמֶמְשָׁלָה וְהַיִּים וְרָע

SECTION 3

Seven double letters serve to signify the antithesis to which human life is exposed. The antithesis of wisdom is foolishness; of wealth, poverty; of fruitfulness, childlessness; of life, death; of dominion, dependence; of peace, war; and of beauty, ugliness.

ג. מִשְׁנָה.

וּבִתְמוּרָה בְּרִבּוּר כַּפְרַ"ת בְּגַ"ד כְּפוּלוֹת שֶׁבַע

תְּמוּרַת עוֹנִי עשֶׁר תְּמוּרַת אִוֶּלֶת חָכְמָה תְּמוּרַת

מֶמְשָׁלָה תְּמוּרַת מָזֶת הַיִּים תְּמוּרַת שְׁמָמָה זֶרַע

כִּיעוּר: חֵן תְּמוּרַת מִלְחָמָה שָׁלוֹם תְּמוּרַת עַבְדוּת

SECTION 4

---

important number, seven, from which descended smaller spheres and which produced again others. He endeavors to show how the ideal became, after numerous emanations, more condensed, palpable and concrete. The whole creation is thus contemplated as a pyramid, terminating in a point at the top with a broad basis. [See Dr. Graetz's Gnosticismus, p. 224.]

The seven double consonants are analogous to the six dimensions: height and depth, East and West, North and South, and the holy temple that stands in the centre, which carries them all.

ד. משנה

מוֹרָח וּמַטָּה מַעֲלָה כַּפְרַ"ת בְּגַ"ד כְּפוּלוֹת שֶׁבַע

בְּאֶמְצַע מְכֻוָּן הַקּוֹרֶשׁ וְהֵיכָל וְדָרוֹם צָפוֹן וּמַעֲרָב

כֻּלָּן: אֶת נוֹשֵׂא וְהוּא

SECTION 5

The double consonants are seven, כפרת בגד and not six, they are seven and not eight; reflect upon this

fact, inquire about it, and make it so evident, that [1] the Creator be acknowledged to be on His throne again.

ה. משנה

שִׁשָּׁה וְ לֹא שִׁבְעָה כַּפְרַ"ת בְּגַ"ד כְּפוּלוֹת שֶׁבַע

וְהַעֲמֹד בָּהֶם נַחֲקוֹר בָּהֶם בָּחוֹן שְׁמוֹנָה וְ לֹא שִׁבְעָה

מְכוֹנוֹ: עַל יוֹצֵר וְהוֹשֵׁב בּוֹרְיוֹ עַל דָּבָר

SECTION 6

The seven double consonants, stamina, having been designed and established, combined, weighed, and changed by God, He

---

[1] Compare Chapter I, Section 3, Note, 8.

formed by them: seven planets in the world, seven days in the year, seven gates, openings of the senses, in man, male and female.

ו. משנה

צָרְפָן חָצְבָן חִקְקָן יְסוֹד כַּפְרַ״ת בְּגַ״ד כְּפוּלוֹת שֶׁבַע

בָּעוֹלָם כּוֹכָבִים שִׁבְעָה בָּהֶם וְצֵר וְהֵמִירָן שְׁקָלָן

זָכָר בַּנֶּפֶשׁ שְׁעָרִים שִׁבְעָה בְּשָׁנָה יָמִים שִׁבְעָה

וּנְקֵבָה:

SECTION 7

The seven planets in the world are: [1] as Saturn, Jupiter, Mars, Sun, Venus, Mercury, Moon. Seven days in the year are the seven days of the week; seven gates in man, male and female, are: two eyes, two ears, two nostrils and the mouth.

ז. משנה

חַמָּה מַאְדִּים צֶדֶק שַׁבְּתַי בָּעוֹלָם כּוֹכָבִים שִׁבְעָה

יְמֵי שִׁבְעָה בְּשָׁנָה יָמִים שִׁבְעָה לְבָנָה כּוֹכָב נֹגַהּ

---

[1] The order of the planets (including the Sun) is stated here according to the Ptolemaic system which was in vogue even among the learned men till the middle of the fifteenth century, namely: Moon, Mercury, Venus, Sun, Mars, Jupiter and Saturn. But this arrangement is undoubtedly an interpolation of a later time, as the author of the book "Yezirah" lived many years before Ptolemy. And indeed Prof. Jo. Friedrich Von Meyer and others of reliable authority had in their copies of "Yezirah" the following order: צדק שבתי לבנה כוכב נוגה חמה מאדים Mars, Jupiter, Saturn, Moon, Mercury, Venus, Sun.

שְׁתֵּי וּנְקֵבָה זָכָר בְּנֶפֶשׁ שְׁעָרִים שִׁבְעָה הַשָּׁבוּעַ

וְהַפֶּה: הָאַף נִקְבֵי שְׁנֵי אָזְנַיִם שְׁתֵּי עֵינַיִם

SECTION 8

FIRST DIVISION. He let the letter ב predominate in wisdom, crowned it, combined one with the other and formed by them: the moon in the world, the first day in the year, and the right eye in man, male and female.

ח משנה.

כֶּתֶר לוֹ וְקָשַׁר בְּהָכְמָה ב׳ אוֹת הִמְלִיךְ. א בָּבָא

רִאשׁוֹן יוֹם בָּעוֹלָם לְבָנָה בָּהֶם וְצָר בָּזֶה זֶה וְצָרְפָן

וּנְקֵבָה: זָכָר בְּנֶפֶשׁ יָמִין וְעַיִן בְּשָׁנָה

SECTION 9

SECOND DIVISION. He let the letter ג predominate in wealth, crowned it, combined one with the other, and formed by them: Mars in the world, the second day in the year, and the right ear in man, male and female.

ט משנה.

כֶּתֶר לוֹ וְקָשַׁר בְּעוֹשֶׁר ג׳ אוֹת הִמְלִיךְ. ב בָּבָא

שֵׁנִי יוֹם בָּעוֹלָם מַאֲדִים בָּהֶם וְצָר מִזֶּה זֶה וְצָרְפָן

וּנְקֵבָה: זָכָר בְּנֶפֶשׁ יָמִין וְ אֹזֶן בְּשָׁנָה

SECTION 10

THIRD DIVISION. He let the letter ד predominate in producibility, crowned it, combined one with the other, and formed by them: the sun in the world, the third day in the year, the right nostril in man, male and female.

משנה י.

כֶּתֶר לוֹ וְקָשַׁר בִּזְרוֹעַ ד׳ אוֹת הַמְלִיךְ .ג בָּבָא

שְׁלִישִׁי יוֹם בָּעוֹלָם חַמָּה בָּהֶם וְצָר בָּזֶה זֶה וְצָרְפָן

וּנְקֵבָה: זָכָר בְּנֶפֶשׁ יָמִין וּנְחִיר בְּשָּׁנָה

SECTION 11

FOURTH DIVISION. He let the letter כ predominate in life, crowned it, combined one with the other, and formed by them: Venus in the world, the fourth day in the year, and the left eye in man, male and female.

י״א משנה.

כֶּתֶר לוֹ וְקָשַׁר בַּחַיִּים כ׳ אוֹת הַמְלִיךְ .ד בָּבָא

רְבִיעִי יוֹם בָּעוֹלָם נוֹגַהּ בָּהֶם וְצָר כָּוֶה זֶה וְצָרְפָן

וּנְקֵבָה: זָכָר בְּנֶפֶשׁ שְׂ מֹאל וְ אֹזֶן בְּשָּׁנָה

SECTION 12

FIFTH DIVISION. He let the letter פ predominate in dominion, crowned it, combined one with the other, and formed by them:

Mercury in the world, the fifth day in the year, and the left ear in man, male and female.

י״ב משנה.

כֶּתֶר לוֹ וְקָשַׁר בְּמֶמְשָׁלָה פּ׳ אוֹת הַמְלִיךְ. ה. בָּבָא

הַחֲמִישִׁי יוֹם בָּעוֹלָם כּוֹכָב בָּהֶם וְצָר בָּזֶה זֶה וְצָרְפָן

וּנְקֵבָה: זָכָר בְּנֶפֶשׁ שְׂמֹאל וְאֹזֶן בְּשָׁנָה

SECTION 13

SIXTH DIVISION. He let the letter ר predominate in peace, crowned it, combined one with the other, and formed by them: Saturn in the world, the sixth day in the year, and the left nostril in man, male and female.

י״ג משנה.

כֶּתֶר לוֹ וְקָשַׁר בְּשָׁלוֹם ר׳ אוֹת הַמְלִיךְ. ו. בָּבָא

שִׁשִּׁי יוֹם בָּעוֹלָם שַׁבְּתַי בָּהֶם וְצָר בָּזֶה זֶה וְצָרְפָן

וּנְקֵבָה: זָכָר בְּנֶפֶשׁ שְׂמֹאל וּנְחִיר בְּשָׁנָה

SECTION 14

SEVENTH DIVISION. He let the letter ת predominate in beauty, crowned it, combined one with the other, and formed by them: Jupiter in the world, the seventh day in the year, and the mouth of man, male and female.

י״ד משנה.

כֶּתֶר לוֹ וְקָשַׁר בָּחֶן בְּ֯ה֯ן ת׳ אוֹת הַמְלִיךְ. ז. בָּבָא

שַׁבָּת יוֹם בָּעוֹלָם צֶדֶק בָּהֶם וְצָר בָּזֶה זֶה וְצָרְפָר

וּנְקֵבָה: זָכָר בְּנֶפֶשׁ וּפֶה בְּשָׁנָה

SECTION 15

By the seven double consonants, כפרת בגד were also designed seven worlds (αἰῶνες), seven heavens, seven lands, (probably climates,) seven seas, (probably around Palestine,) seven rivers, seven deserts, seven days a week, seven weeks from Passover to Pentecost, there is a cycle of seven years, the seventh is the release year, and after seven release years is jubilee. Hence, God loves the number seven under the whole heaven. [1] (In the whole nature.)

ט״ו משרה

.

שִׁבְעָה שֶׁבְּקָקִין כַּפְרַ״ת בְּגַ״ד בְּפוּלוֹת שֶׁבַע

יָמִים שִׁבְעָה אֲרָצוֹת שִׁבְעָה רְקִיעִין שִׁבְעָה עוֹלָמוֹת

שִׁבְעָה יָמִים שִׁבְעָה מִדְבָּרוֹת שִׁבְעָה נְהָרִית שִׁבְעָה

יוֹבְלוֹת שִׁבְעָה שְׁמִיטִין שִׁבְנָה שָׁנִים שִׁבְעָה שְׁבוּעוֹת

הַשָּׁמַיִם: כָּל תַּחַת הַשְּׁבִיעִיּוֹת אֶת הַבַּב לְפִיכָךְ

---

[1] Philo (Allegor 1, 42,) after having called attention to the fact that the heptade is to be found in many biblical laws, in the vowels of the Greek language, in the gamut and in the organs of the human body, exclaims, similar to our author: "The whole nature exults in the heptade!"

SECTION 16

Two stones build two houses, three stones build six houses, four build twenty-four houses, five build one hundred and twenty houses, six build seven hundred and twenty houses and seven build five thousand and forty [1] houses. From thence further go and reckon what the mouth cannot express and the ear cannot hear.

משנה ט״ז.

אֲבָנִים שְׁלֹשׁ בָּתִּים שְׁנֵי בּוֹנוֹת אֲבָנִים שְׁתֵּי

אַרְבָּעָה בּוֹנוֹת אֲבָנִים אַרְבַּע בָּתִּים שִׁשָּׁה בּוֹנוֹת

וְעֶשְׂרִים מֵאָה בּוֹנוֹת אֲבָנִים חָמֵשׁ בָּתִּים וְעֶשְׂרִים

וְעֶשְׂרִים מֵאוֹת שֶׁבַע בּוֹנוֹת אֲבָנִים שֵׁשׁ בָּתִּים

אֲלָפִים חֲמֵשֶׁת בּוֹנוֹת אֲבָנִים שֶׁבַע בָּתִּים

וַחֲשׁוֹב צֵא וְאֵילֵךְ מִכָּאן בָּתִּים וְאַרְבָּעִים (וארבע)

יְכוֹלָה הָ אֹזֶן וְאֵין לְדַבֵּר יְכוֹלָה הַפֶּה שֶׁאֵין מַה

לִשְׁמוֹעַ:

---

[1] The rule for permutation is as follows: (n--1) n. 1 x 2 x 3 x 4 x 5 x 6 x 7=5040. In our edition it reads: בתים וארבע אלפים חמשת Five thousand and four houses, which is obviously a mistake, it should read: 5040 houses. בתים וארבעם אלפים חמשת.

CHAPTER V.

SECTION 1

THE twelve simple letters ע״צ״ק ל״נ״ם ח״ט״י ה״ו״ז symbolize, as it were, the organs of speaking, thinking, walking, seeing, hearing, working, coition, smelling, sleep, anger, swallowing and laughing.

פרק חמישי.

משנה א.

עצ״ק לנ״ם חט״י הו״ז פְּשׁוּטוֹת עֶשְׂרֵה שְׁתֵּים

מַעֲשֶׂה שְׁמִיעָה רְאִיָּה הִלּוּךְ הִרְהוּר שִׂיחָה יְסוֹדָן

שְׂחוֹק: לְעִיטָה רוֹגֶז שֵׁינָה רֵיחַ תַּשְׁמִישׁ

SECTION 2

The twelve simple consonants ע״צ״ק ל״נ״ם ח״ט״י ה״ו״ז symbolize also twelve oblique points: east height, north east, east depth, south height, south east, south depth, west height, south west, west depth, north height, north west, north depth. They grew wider and wider to all eternity, and these are the boundaries of the world.

משנה ב.

עצ״ק לנ״ם חט״י הו״ז פְּשׁוּטוֹת עֶשְׂרֵה שְׁתֵּים

מִזְרָחִית גְּבוּל אֲלַכְסוֹן גְּבוּלֵי עָשָׂר שְׁנֵים יְסוֹדָן

תַּחְתִּית מִזְרָחִית גְּבוּל צְפוֹנִית מִזְרָחִית גְּבוּל רוֹמִית

גְּבוּל יְמִזְרָחִית דְּרוֹמִית גְּבוּל רוֹמִית דְּרוֹמִית גְּבוּל

גְּבוּל רוֹמִית מַעֲרָבִית גְּבוּל תַּחְתִּית דְּרוֹמִית

גְּבוּל תַּחְתִּית מַעֲרָבִית גְּבוּל דְּרוֹמִית מַעֲרָבִית

צְפוֹנִית גְּבוּל מַעֲרָבִית צְפוֹנִית גְּבוּל רוֹמִית צְפוֹנִית

הֵן וְהֵן עַד עֲדֵי עַד וְ הִילְכִין וּמִתְרַחֲבִין תַּחְתִּית

עוֹלָם: גְּבוּלוֹת

SECTION 3

The twelve simple letters ע״צ״ק ל״נ״ם ח״ט״י ה״ו״ז stamina, having been designed, established, combined, weighed and changed by God, He performed by them: twelve constellations in the world, twelve months in the year, and twelve leaders (organs) in the human body, male and female.

ג. משנה

עצ״ק לנ״ם חט״י הו״ז פְּשׁוּטוֹת עֶשְׂרֵה שְׁתֵּים

בָּהֶם וְצָר וְהֵמִירָן שְׁקָלָן צְרָפָן חֲצָבָן הֲקָקָן יְסוֹדָן

חֳדָשִׁים עָשָׂר שְׁנֵים בָּעוֹלָם מַזָּלוֹת עֶשְׂרֵה שְׁתֵּים

וּנְקֵבָה: זָכָר בְּנֶפֶשׁ מַנְהִיגִים עָשָׂר שְׁנֵים בַּשָּׁנָה

SECTION 4

The twelve constellations in the world are: Aries, Taurus, Gemini, Cancer, Leo, Virgo, Libra, Scorpio, Sagitarius, Capricornus, Aquarius and Pisces. The twelve months of the year are: Nisan, Iyar, Sivan, Tamus, Ab, Elul, Tishri, Marcheshvan, Kislev, Teves, Schevat and Adar. The twelve organs of the human body are: two hands, two feet, two kidneys, gall, small intestines, liver, gullet [1] or esophagus, stomach and milt.

ד. משנה

טְאוֹמוֹם שׁוֹר טָלֶה בָּעוֹלָם מַזָּלוֹת עֶשְׂרֵה שְׁתֵּים

דְּלִי גְּדִי קֶשֶׁת עַקְרָב מֹאזְנַיִם בְּתוּלָה אַרְיֵה סַרְטָן

סִיוָן אִיָּיר נִיסָן בְּשָׁנָה הֳחָדָשִׁים עָשָׂר שְׁנֵים דָגִים:

אֲדָר: שְׁבָט טֵבֵת כִּסְלֵו חֶשְׁוָן תִּשְׁרֵי אֱלוּל אָב תַּמּוּז

יָדַיִם שְׁתֵּי וּנְקֵבָה זָכָר בְּנֶפֶשׁ מַנְהִיגִים עָשָׂר שְׁנֵים

(קוֹרְקוֹבֶן) כָּבֵד דַּקִין מָרָה כְּלָיוֹת שְׁתֵּי רַגְלַיִם שְׁתֵּי

טְחוֹל: קֵבָה גַּרְגֶּרֶת

SECTION 5

First Part

---

[1] I read גרגרת instead of קורקובן for two reasons. In the first place, the same thing is mentioned afterwards, and in the second place, it is proved by the expression לעיטה that the author meant גרגרת and not קורקובן.

FIRST DIVISION. God let the letter ה predominate in speaking, crowned it, combined one with the other, and formed by them: Aries (the Ram) in the world, the month Nisan in the year, and the right foot of the human body, male and female.

ה. מִשְׁנָה

מֵהָא א׳ בָּבָא. וְקָשַׁר בְּשִׂיחָה ה׳ אוֹת הִמְלִיךְ לוֹ

וּבִיסָן בָּעוֹלָם טָלֶה בָּהֶם וְצָר בָּזֶה זֶה וְצָרְפָן כֶּתֶר

וּנְקֵבָה: זָכָר בְּנֶפֶשׁ יָמִין וְרֶגֶל בְּשָׁנָה

SECTION 6

SECOND DIVISION. He let the letter ו predominate in thinking, crowned it, combined one with the other, and formed by them: Taurus (the Bull) in the world, the month Iyar in the year and the right kidney of the human body, male and female.

ו. מִשְׁנָה

מֵהָא ב׳ בָּבָא. וְקָשַׁר בְּהִרְהוּר י׳ אוֹת הִמְלִיךְ לוֹ

וְאִיָּיר בָּעוֹלָם שׁוֹר בָּהֶם וְצָר בָּזֶה זֶה וְצָרְפָן כֶּתֶר

וּנְקֵבָה: זָכָר בְּנֶפֶשׁ יָמֵנִית וְכוּלְיָא בְּשָׁנָה

SECTION 7

THIRD DIVISION. He let the letter ז predominate in walking, crowned it, combined one with the other, and formed by them: Gemini (the Twins) in the world, the month Sivan in the year, and the left foot of the human body, male and female.

משנה ז.

מֵהָא ג' בְּבָא. אוֹת הַמְלִיךְ ז' בְּהִלּוּךְ וְקָשַׁר לוֹ

וְסִינָן בְּעוֹלָם בְּאוֹמִים בָּהֶם וְצָר בָּזֶה זֶה וְצָרְפָן כֶּתֶר

וּנְקֵבָה: זָכָר בְּנֶפֶשׁ שְׂמֹאל וְרֶגֶל בְּשָׁנָה

SECTION 8

Second Part

FIRST DIVISION. He let the letter ח predominate in seeing, crowned it, combined one with the other, and formed by them: Cancer (the Crab) in the world, the month Tamus in the year, and the right hand of the human body, male and female.

משנה ח.

הַשְּׁנִיָּה מִן א' בְּבָא. אוֹת הַמְלִיךְ ח' בִּרְאִיָּה וְקָשַׁר

בְּעוֹלָם סַרְטָן בָּהֶם וְצָר בָּזֶה זֶה וְצָרְפָן כֶּתֶר לוֹ

וּנְקֵבָה: זָכָר בְּנֶפֶשׁ יָמִין וְיָד בְּשָׁנָה וְתַמּוּז

SECTION 9

SECOND DIVISION. He let the letter ט predominate in hearing, crowned it, combined one with the other, and formed by them: Leo (the Lion) in the world, the month Ab in the year, and the left kidney of the human body, male and female.

משנה ט.

בְּשָׁמַיִ׳ עה ט׳ אות הַמְלִיךְ. הַשְּׁנִיָּה מִן ב׳ בָּבָא

בְּעוֹלָם אַרְיֵה בָּהֶם וְצָר בָּזֶה וּצְרָפָן כֶּתֶר לוֹ וְקָשַׁר

וּנְקֵבָה: זָכָר בְּנֶפֶשׁ שְׂמָאלִית וְכוּלְיָא בְּשָׁנָה וְאָב

SECTION 10

THIRD DIVISION. He let the letter י predominate in working, crowned it, combined one with the other, and formed by them: Virgo (the Virgin) in the world, the month Elul in the year, and the left hand of the human body, male and female.

י. משנה

וְקָשַׁר בְּמַעֲשֶׂה י׳ אוֹת הַמְלִיךְ. הַשְּׁנִיָּה מִן ג׳ בָּבָא

בְּעוֹלָם בְּתוּלָה בָּהֶם וְצָר בָּזֶה וּצְרָפָן כֶּתֶר לוֹ

וּנְקֵבָה: זָכָר בְּנֶפֶשׁ שׂ מֹאל וְיַד בְּשָׁנָה וֶאֱלוּל

SECTION 11

Third Part

FIRST DIVISION. He let the letter ל predominate in coition, crowned it, combined one with the other, and formed by them: Libra (the Balance) in the world, the month Tishri in the year, and the gall of the human body, male and female.

י״א משנה.

בְּתַשְׁמִישׁ ל׳ אוֹת הַמְלִיךְ. הַשְּׁלִישִׁית מִן א׳ בָּבָא

מֹאזְנַיִם בָּהֶם וְצָר בָּזֶה וּצְרָפָן כֶּתֶר לוֹ וְקָשַׁר

וּנְקֵבָה: זָכָר בְּנֶפֶשׁ וּמָרָה בְּשָׁנָה וְתִשְׁרֵי בָּעוֹלָם

SECTION 12

SECOND DIVISION. He let the letter נ predominate in smelling, crowned it, combined one with the other, and formed by them: Scorpio (the Scorpion) in the world, the month Marcheshvan in the year, and the small intestines of the human body, male and female.

י״ב משנה.

הַשְּׁלִישִׁית מִן ב׳ בָּבָא. וְקָשַׁר בְּרֵיהַ נ׳ אוֹת הִמְלִיךְ

בָּעוֹלָם עַקְרָב בָּהֶם וְצָר בָּזֶה וְצֵרְפָן כֶּתֶר לוֹ

וּנְקֵבָה: זָכָר בְּנֶפֶשׁ וְדַקִּין בְּשָׁנָה וּמַרְחֶשְׁוָן

SECTION 13

THIRD DIVISION. He let the letter ס predominate in sleep, crowned it, combined one with the other, and formed by them: Sagittarius (the Archer) in the world, the month Kislev in the year, and the stomach of the human body, male and female.

י״ג משנה.

הַשְּׁלִישִׁית מִן ג׳ בָּבָא. בְּשָׁנָה ס׳ אוֹת הִמְלִיךְ

בָּעוֹלָם גְּדִי בָּהֶם וְצָר בָּזֶה וְצֵרְפָן כֶּתֶר לוֹ וְקָשַׁר

וּנְקֵבָה: זָכָר בְּנֶפֶשׁ וְכָבֵד בְּשָׁנָה טֵבֵת

SECTION 14

Fourth Part

FIRST DIVISION. He let the letter ע predominate in anger, crowned it, combined one with the other, and formed by them: Capricornus (the Goat) in the world, the month Teves in the year, and the liver in the human body, male and female.

י"ד משנה.

בְּרוֹגֶז ע' אוֹת הִמְלִיךְ. הָרְבִיעִית מִן א' בָּבָה

בָּעוֹלָם גְּדִי בָּהֶם וְצָר בֵּהּ זֶה וְצָרְפָן כֶּתֶר לוֹ וְקָשַׁר

וּנְקֵבָה: זָכָר בְּנֶפֶשׁ וְכָבֵד בְּשָׁנָה טֵבֵת

SECTION 15

SECOND DIVISION. He let the letter צ predominate in swallowing, crowned it, combined one with the other, and formed by them: Aquarius (the Water-man) in the world, the month Schwat in the year, and the esophagus of the human body, male and female.

ט"ו משנה.

בִּלְעִיטָח צ' אוֹת הִמְלִיךְ. הָרְבִיעִית מִן ב' בָּבָא

בָּעוֹלָם דְּלִי בָּהֶם בָּזֶה זֶה וְצָרְפָן כֶּתֶר לוֹ וְקָשַׁר

וּנְקֵבָה: זָכָר בְּנֶפֶשׁ וְגַרְגֶּרֶת (נְקוּרְקְבָן) בְּשָׁנָה וּשְׁבָט

SECTION 16

THIRD DIVISION. He let the letter ק predominate in laughing, crowned it, combined one with the other, and formed by them: Pisces (the Fishes) in the world, the month Adar in the year, and the milt of the human body, male and female.

He made them as a conflict, drew them up like a wall; and set one against the other as in warfare.

ט״ז משנה.

בִּשְׂחוֹק ק׳ אוֹת הִמְלִיךְ. הָרְבִיעִית מִן ג׳ בָּבָא

בָּצוֹלָם דָּגִים בָּהֶם וְצָר בָּזֶה זֶה וְצֵרְפָן כֶּתֶר לוֹ וְקָשַׁר

כְּמִין עָשְׂאָן וּבִקְבָה זָכָר בְּנֶפֶשׁ וּטְחוֹל בְּשָׁנָה וְעֶדֶר

מִלְחָמָה: כְּמִין עָרְכָן חוֹמָה כְּמִין סִידְרָן *עָרֵיבָה

מְרִינָה: אוֹ מְרִיבָה נ״א (*

CHAPTER VI.

SECTION 1

THESE are the three mothers or the first elements, א״מ״ש from which emanated three progenitors; primitive air, water and fire, and from which emanated as their offspring, three progenitors and their offspring, namely: the seven planets and their hosts, and the twelve oblique points.

פרק ששי.

א. משנה

שָׁלֹשׁ מֵהֶם וְיָצְאוּ אֲ״מֶ״ש אִמּוֹת שָׁלֹשׁ הֵם עָלוּ

שְׁלֹשָׁה תּוֹלְדוֹת וּמֵאָבוֹת וְאֵשׁ וּמַיִם אַוִּיר וְהֵם אָבוֹת

וְצִבְאוֹתֵיהֶם כּוֹכָבִים וְשִׁבְעָה וְתוֹלְדוֹתֵיהֶם אָבוֹת

אֲלַכְסוֹן: גְּבוּלֵי עֶשֶׂר וּשְׁנֵים

SECTION 2

To confirm this there are faithful witnesses; the world, year and man, the twelve, the Equipoise, the heptade, which God regulates like the Dragon, [1] (Tali) sphere and the heart.

---

[1] Some maintain that by the expression Tali is understood the constellation Draco or Dragon, which is a very large constellation extending for a great length from East to West; beginning at the tail which lies half way between the Pointers and the Pole Star, and

ב. משנה

גֶּפֶשׁ שָׁנָה בָּעוֹלָם נֶאֱמָנִים עֵדִים לַדָּבָר רְאָיָה

כְּתָלִי וּפִקְדָן וּשְׁלֹשָׁה וְשִׁבְעָה חָק עָשָׂר וּשְׁנֵים

וָלֵב: וְנַלְנַל

SECTION 3

The first elements א"מ"ש are air, water and fire; the fire is above, the water below, and a breath of air establishes the balance among them. For an illustration may serve, that the fire carries the water is the phonetic character of מ which is mute and ש is hissing like fire, there is א among them, a breath of air which places them in <u>equilibrium</u>. [1]

ג. משנה

---

winding round between the Great and Little Bear by a continued succession of bright stars from 5 to 10 degrees asunder, it coils round under the feet of the Little Bear, sweeps round the pole of the ecliptic, and terminates in a trapezium formed by four conspicuous stars from 30 to 35 degrees from North Pole. Dr. Steinshneider (see Magazin fuer Literatur des Auslandes, 1845) and Dr. Cassel (in his commentary to the book entitled Kusari,) maintain that the ancient Jewish astronomers signified by the word Tali, not the constellation Draco, but the line which joins together the two points in which the orbit of the moon intercepts the ecliptic (Dragon's head and tail). Dr. Cassel is of the opinion that our author meant here, probably the invisible, celestial or universal axis that carries the whole Universe.

[1] Our author means to say that the water has a great disposition to unite itself with the caloric, thus for instance is the fire latent in steam, but the air equipoises them.

לְמַעֲלָה אֵשׁ וּמַיִם אֵשׁ אֲוִיר אֶ״מַ״שׁ אִמּוֹת שָׁלֹשׁ

וְסִימָן בִּנְתַיִם מַכְרִיעַ חָק רוּחַ וַאֲוִיר לְמַטָּה וּמַיִם

שׁוֹרֶקֶת שׁ׳ דּוֹמֶמֶת מ׳ הַמַּיִם אֶת נוֹשֵׂא הָאֵשׁ לְדָבָר

בִּנְתַיִם: מַכְרִיעַ חָק רוּחַ אֲוִיר א׳

SECTION 4

Dragon (Tali) is in the world like a king upon his throne, the sphere is in the year like a king in the empire, and the heart is in the human body like a king [1] in war.

ד. משנה

כְּמֶלֶךְ בְּשָׁנָה גַלְגַּל כִּסְאוֹ עַל בְּמֶלֶךְ בָּעוֹלָם תָּלִי

בְּמִלְחָמָה: כְּמֶלֶךְ בְּנֶפֶשׁ לֵב *בִּמְדִינָה

חוֹמָה: עַל נ״א (*

SECTION 5

God has also set the one over against the other; the good against the evil, and the evil against the good; the good proceeds from the good, and the evil from the evil; the good purifies the bad, and the bad the good; the good is preserved for the good, and the evil for the bad ones.

ה. משנה

---

[1] The meaning is, as God is the centre of the Universe, so have the macrocosm, the seasons and temperature and the microcosm, their centres receiving power from the principal centre to regulate and rule.

לְעֻמַּת טוֹב אֱלֹהִים עָשָׂה זֶה לְעֻמַּת זֶה אֶת גַּם

הַטּוֹב מֵרָע רָע מִטּוֹב טוֹב לְעֻמַּת רָע רָע

טוֹבָה הַטּוֹב אֶת מַבְחִין וְהָרַע הָרַע אֶת מַבְחִין

לְרָעִים: שְׁמוּרָה וְרָעָה לַטּוֹבִים שְׁמוּרָה

SECTION 6

There are three of which every one of them stands by itself; one is in the affirmative, the other in the negative and one equalizes them.

ו. משנה

וְאֶחָד מְזַכֶּה אֶחָד עוֹמֵד לְבַדּוֹ אֶחָד כָּל שְׁלֹשָׁה

בֵּנְתַיִם: מַכְרִיעַ וְאֶחָד מְחַיֵּב

SECTION 7

There are seven of which three are against three, and one places them in equilibrium. There are twelve which are all the time at war; three of them produce love, and three hatred, three are animators and three destroyers.

ז. משנה

בֵּנְתַיִם בַּכְרִיעַ וְאֶחָד שְׁלֹשָׁה מוּל שְׁלֹשָׁה שִׁבְעָה

אוֹהֲבִים שְׁלֹשָׁה בַּמִּלְחָמָה: עוֹמְדִין עָשָׂר וּשְׁנַיִם

מְמִיתִים: וּשְׁלֹשָׁה מְחַיִּים שְׁלֹשָׁה שׂוֹנְאִים שְׁלֹשָׁה

SECTION 8

The three that produce love are the heart and the ears; the three that produce hatred are the liver, the gall and the tongue; the three animators are the two nostrils and the milt; and the three destroyers are the mouth and the two openings of the body; and God, the faithful King, rules over all from His holy habitation to all eternity. He is one above three, three are above seven, seven above twelve, and all are linked together.

ח. משנה

שׂוֹנְאִים שְׁלשָׁה וְהָאָזְנַיִם הַלֵב אוֹהֲבִים שְׁלשָׁה

הָאַף נִקְבֵי שְׁנֵי מְהַיִּים שְׁלשָׁח וְהַלָשׁוֹן הַמָרָה הַכָּבֵד

וְאֵל וְהַפֶּה הַנְקָבִים שְׁנֵי מְמִיתִים וּשְׁלשָׁה וְהַטְחִי ל

עַד עֲדִי עַד קָדְשׁוֹ מִמְעוֹן בְּכֻלָם מוֹשֵׁל נֶאֱמָן מֶלֶךְ

שִׁבְעָה שִׁבְעָה גַבֵּי עַל שְׁלשָׁה שְׁלשָׁה גַבֵּי עַל אֶחָד

בָּזֶה: זֶה אֲדוּקִים וְכֻלָם עָשָׂר שְׁנֵים גַבֵּי עַל

SECTION 9

There [1] are twenty-two letters by which the I am, Yah, the Lord of hosts, Almighty and Eternal, designed, formed and created by

---

[1] The substance of this Mishnah is mentioned in the Talmud treatise Berachoth, p. 55, a. It reads there:
חיה יודע רב אמר יחידח רב אמר
וארץ: שמיס בהן שנבראו אותיות לצרף בצלעל

three Sepharim, His whole world, and formed by them creatures and all those that will be formed in time to come.

ט. משנה

אֱהָיֶה חָקַק הָקֵק שֶׁבָּהֶן אוֹתִיוֹת וּשְׁתַּיִם עֶשְׂרִים הֵם אוּ

מֵהֶם וְעָשָׂה אֱ לֹהִים יְהֹוָה שַׁדַּי אֵל צְבָאוֹת יְהֹוָה יָהּ

בָּהֶם וְצָר עוֹלָמוֹ כָּל אֵת מֵהֶם וּבָרָא סְפָרִים שְׁלֹשָׁה

לָצוּר: הֶעָתִיד כָּל וְאֵת הַיְצוּר כָּל אֵת

SECTION 10

When [1] the patriarch Abraham comprehended the great truism, revolved it in his mind, conceived it perfectly, made careful investigations and profound inquiries, pondered upon it and succeeded in contemplations, the Lord of the Universe appeared to him, called him his friend, made with him a covenant between the ten fingers of his hands, which is the covenant of the tongue, [2] and the covenant between the ten

---

"Rab Jehudah stated in the name of Rab, that Bezalel understood to combine letters by which heaven and earth were created." To this the commentator Rashi adds: "as it is taught in the book Yezirah." It is undoubtedly certain that the book Yezirah, or a cosmogony as it is represented there, was known to Rab, who was a disciple of Jehudah Hanasi, during the second part of the second century. (C. E.) See treatise Berachoth, p. 55 a, where the commentator Rashi referred to the book Yezirah.

[1] This whole paragraph is an interpolation of an unknown hand, as it can be easily proved.

[2] I have translated according to the reading of Rabbi Judah Halevi. The reading of Rabbi Luria is as follows:

אותיות ושתים עשרים וקשר

toes of his feet, which is the covenant of circumcision, and said of him: "Before I formed thee in the belly I knew thee." (Jer. I, 5.)

י. משנה

וְחָצַב וְחָקַק וְרָאָה וְהִבִּיט אָבִינוּ אַבְרָהָם וּכְשֶׁהֵבִין

אוֹהֲבִי וְקִרְאוֹ ה' כֹּל אָדוֹן עָלָיו נִגְלָה בְּיָדוֹ וְעָלְתָה

בְּרִית וְהוּא יָדָיו אֶצְבָּעוֹת עֶשֶׂר בֵּין בְּרִית לוֹ וְכָרַת

הַמִּילָה בְּרִית וְהוּא רַגְלָיו אֶצְבָּעוֹת עֶשֶׂר וּבֵין הַלָּשׁוֹן

*יְדַעְתִּיךָ: בַּבֶּטֶן אֶצָּרְךָ בְּטֶרֶם עָלָיו וְקָרָא

יְסוֹנֵץ אֶת לוֹ וְנִגְלָה בִּלְשׁוֹנוֹ אוֹת יוֹת וּשְׁתַּיִם עֶשְׂרִים וְקָשַׁר נ"א (*

עֲשֶׂרֶת בִּשְׁתֵּים נֶהֱנָן בְּשִׁבְעָה בָּעָרָן בְּרוּחַ רָעַשָׁן כָּאֵשׁ דָּלְקָן בַּמַּיִם מָשְׁכָן

מַנְלוֹת:

יצירה: ספר וסליק. פרקא סליק

בערן בויח רעשן באש דלקן במים משכן סודו את לו וגילח בלשונו
עשר בשנים נהגין בשבעה

"He fastened twenty-two letters on his tongue and revealed to him His mystery, He drew them by water, kindled them by fire and thundered them by the wind, He lighted them by seven, and rules them by twelve constellations." Pistor. renders it: "Tranat per aquam, accendit in igne grandine signavit in äere. Disposuit cum septem et gubernavit cum duodecim." Postellus' version is: "Attraxit eam in aqua, accendit in spiritu, inflammavit in septem aptatum cum duodecim signis." Meyer translates it: "Er zog sie mit Wasser, zündet sie an mit Feuer, erregte sie mit Geist, vebrannte sie mit sieben, goes sie aus mit den swoelf Gestirnen."

GLOSSARY OF RABBINICAL WORDS

א

אָדַק v. To adhere, cohere. VI, 8.

אֲדֵר n. [Syriac אאר, Greek ἀήρ] Air. II.

אוֹת n. Sign, letter; אוֹתִיּוֹת, יְסוֹד fundamental letters. I, 1.

אֵילָךְ adv. וְאֵילָךְ מִבָּאן hinc et ulterius; from now further. IV 16

אֵלּוּ. These. Equals the biblical אֵלֶּה.VI. 1.

אֲלַכְסוֹן adj. [Greek λόξον] Oblique, diagonal direction. V, 2.

אֶמְצָע n. Middle. centre. I, 2.

ב

בּוּרִי n. Clearness, perspicuity. I, 3. בּוּרְיוֹ עַל דָּבָר וְהַעֲמֵד and put the subject in a clear point of view.

בָּבָא n. Division. V, 6.

בִּינוֹתַם or בֵּנְתַּיִם Composed of שֶׁתְּוַם בֵּין, omitting שׁ between them. I, 1. [See Duke's Sprache der Mischnah, p. 68.]

ג

גָּב n. Back. גַּבֵּי עַג upon the back id est, upon or above. VI, 8.

גוּף n. Body, substance II, 6.

גַּלְגַּל n. Circle, celestial orb, or sphere. II, 4.

ד

דִּבּוּר n. Word. I, 8.

ה

הִרְהֵר v. Think, muse. meditate, reflect. I, 7.

הִרְהוּר n. Reflection, meditation. V, 1.

ז

זְכוּת n. Innocence, purity, godliness, merit. II, 1.

ח

חוֹכָה n. Misdeed, trespass. II, 1.

חָזַר v. To return, to turn one's self round. II, 5.

חֲלִילָה n. Rotation; from חָלל to dance round. II, 5.

ט

טְחוֹל n. Milt, spleen. V, 4.

כ

כָּאן or בַּאן adv. Here, there; מִכָּאן thence, from thence. IV, 16.

כּוֹכָב n. Star; especially the planet Mercury. IV, 7.

כִּין piel כֵּין v. Direct; מְכֻוָּן directed, situated. I, 2.

כִּיעוּר n. Ugliness. IV, 3.

כַּךְ or לְכָךְ adv. So, thus. I, 7.

כָּרַע Hiph. הִכְרִיעַ v. To intervene in any thing, to mediate the peace, accomodate a quarrel. II, 1.

ל

לְעִימָה n. Eating, swallowing. V, 1.

לְפִיכָךְ adv. Composed of the words לְפִי and כָּךְ. According to that, therefore. IV, 15.

מ

מַאֲדִים n. The planet Mars. IV, 7.

מִדָּה n. Measure, quality, divine attribute. I, 4.

מִשְׁנָה n. Doctrine, lesson, paragraph.

מַזָּלוֹת n. Constellations; especially the twelve signs of the Zodiac. V, 3. מַזָּל טוֹב a happy constellation.

כְּמִין adv. It is a particle like כ, as; it is added the word מִין kind, denoting: as a kind of, like, as. II, 4.

מֵימַר v. Chald. inf. מַאֲמַר or מֵמַר. To speak, command. II, 5.

מַמָּשׁ n. Substance, reality. II, 5.

מַעֲוִיבָה n. Rampart, a floor, pavement. I, 8.

מָרָה n. Gall. V, 4

מִתְנַהֵן See נָהַן. IV, 1.

נ

נָהַן v. With a ב following after it, signifies: to make use of any thing. IV, 1.

נוֹנָה n. The planet Venus. IV, 7.

נָעַץ v. Chald. Stick in, fasten, conjoin, connect. I, 6.

נָקָב n. Opening. IV, 8.

ס

סָדַר v. Arrange. V, 16.

סִימָן n. σημεῖον Sign, illustration. II, 4. [See Geiger's Lesestücke der Mishnah, p. 121.]

סְלִיק n. Finished; the end (of a book or chapter.)

ע

עֲרֵיבָה n. Contention, rivalry. V, 5.

עָתִיד n. Future. II, 2.

פ

פֶּרֶק n. Chapter, section.

פָּשׁוּם adj. Divested of clothes, undressed, simple. I, 8.

צ

צֶרֶק n. The planet Jupiter. IV, 7.

צְפִיָּח n. Appearance. I, 5.

צָרַף v. Refine, melt together, connect, combine. II, 2.

ק

קָבַע v. To fix, to fasten. I, 8. II, 3.

קֵיבָח or קֵבָה n. Stomach. V, 4.

קוּרְקְבָן or קֻרְקְבָן n. Stomach. V, 4.

ר

רְאָיָה n. Argument, evidence. VI, 2.

רְאִיָה n. Sight. V, 1.

רְוִיָה n. Redundancy of water, moistness. III. 4.

רֵיחַ v. Smell. V, 1.

ש

שַׁבְחָאִי n. The planet Saturn. IV, 7.

שִׂיחָה n. Speaking. V, 1.

שְׁמִיעָה n. Hearing. V, 1.

שֵׁרֵת v. To serve. I, 8.

ת

תְּלִי n. The constellation Draco or Dragon. VI, 2.

תַּשְׁמִישׁ n. Coition. V, 1.

תָּפַם or תָּפַשׂ v. To seize, to take hold of.

www.ingramcontent.com/pod-product-compliance
Lightning Source LLC
Chambersburg PA
CBHW051553010526
44118CB00022B/2693